THE SELF-CONFIDENCE JOURNAL

THE
SELF-
CONFIDENCE
JOURNAL

Prompts and Practices to Overcome Self-Doubt and Improve Self-Esteem

DAVID SHANLEY, PsyD

ROCKRIDGE
PRESS

To my son, Jack, who has already challenged my self-confidence
and inspired me to grow in more ways than I could imagine.

For general information on our other products and services or to obtain technical support, please contact our Customer Care Department within the United States at (866) 744-2665, or outside the United States at (510) 253-0500.

Rockridge Press publishes its books in a variety of electronic and print formats. Some content that appears in print may not be available in electronic books, and vice versa.

TRADEMARKS: Rockridge Press and the Rockridge Press logo are trademarks or registered trademarks of Callisto Media Inc. and/or its affiliates, in the United States and other countries, and may not be used without written permission. All other trademarks are the property of their respective owners. Rockridge Press is not associated with any product or vendor mentioned in this book.

Interior and Cover Designer: Jill Lee
Art Producer: Hannah Dickerson
Editor: Carolyn Abate
Production Editor: Jael Fogle
Production Manager: David Zapanta

Author photo courtesy of John Farrell

Paperback ISBN: 978-1-63878-097-7
eBook ISBN: 978-1-63878-313-8
R0

CONTENTS

THIS JOURNAL BELONGS TO

INTRODUCTION

Welcome to *The Self-Confidence Journal*. This journal is intended to help you boost your self-confidence and overcome nagging anxiety and doubts that may be holding you back. Whether you are young or old, an expert or a novice, you have likely picked up this book because you are tired of feeling stuck, hopeless, or anxious about yourself and your effectiveness in the world. Whether you are taking on a new job, relationship, relocation, or social activity, a boost of self-confidence can go a long way toward making the experience more enjoyable and meaningful. This journal will guide you through different thought patterns and strategies to help you move forward with your life.

Self-confidence is knowing—not just believing—that you are competent, worthy, and able to adapt, learn, and grow to go after the things you want in life. Self-confidence does not mean that you will always excel in every situation; rather, even in situations that are challenging, you believe you will manage the situation effectively and cope with difficulties as they arise.

Self-confidence is a combination of trust, compassion, courage, and thoughtfulness that promotes healthy behavior and values-driven action. It could include an ability to laugh at one's mistakes and a willingness to try something new and challenging.

A lack of self-confidence often comes from childhood, either from messages we received or negative experiences that shaped our beliefs about ourselves.

Self-esteem and self-confidence are closely related. The more positive you feel about yourself, the more confident you feel in the world. Overconfidence is not the same as self-confidence; it often acts as a front people put up to protect themselves from having to be vulnerable or letting others see their flaws.

I am a licensed psychologist, specializing in the treatment of anxiety disorders. I regularly discuss the ideas, prompts, and exercises in this book to help clients heal from past difficulties and bolster themselves to take on new challenges.

The structure of this book follows the principles of Acceptance and Commitment Therapy (ACT): understanding oneself; identifying goals; practicing acceptance, mindfulness, and calming techniques; letting go of negative thoughts; and taking action that feels uncomfortable (exposure). It is fine to flip through the book to the sections that feel most relevant to your life.

However, if you find yourself struggling with anxiety, depression, or other mental health issues, I encourage you to talk to a professional. There is a Resources section at the end of this book (page 167) for guidance on finding help.

You will get the most out of this book by setting aside at least a couple of times per week to work on an entry or exercise. Repetition and practice are key to overcoming anxiety and building confidence. Remember, the action has to come first, and the feelings of confidence will come from the doing.

How to use this journal with *The Self-Confidence Workbook*

While I believe this journal has value on its own, it can also serve as a companion to The Self-Confidence Workbook. *You will find that the more you work on these issues, especially the things that are uncomfortable, the easier it gets over time.*

The workbook tends to focus more on exercises and what to do to build self-confidence. This journal, conversely, is more about personal reflections, getting in touch with and giving space to your emotions, and processing your journey of building confidence as you go through it. I believe reflection and emotional processing are critical aspects of building self-confidence, so rest assured that there is value to this journal in building your confidence.

If you have the workbook, I recommend you go through the chapters and exercises there, but also make sure you pull out this journal each week to do at least one or two reflections and check in with yourself about how the process is going.

Look within. Within is the fountain of Good.

– MARCUS AURELIUS, MEDITATIONS

1

UNDERSTANDING WHERE YOU ARE

The goal of this section is to help you understand your own level of self-confidence, the areas where it is strong, and places it is lacking. This process might cue up some feelings of discomfort and shame. The good news is that by being honest with yourself, you are already doing both an emotional exposure and an important goal-setting exercise. This will be useful in assessing how self-confidence impacts you and what you can do differently to grow.

WHERE DO YOU FEEL CONFIDENT?

As with anything in life, the only way to build upon something is to start where you're at. Where do you feel most confident in your life? Where do you feel least confident? Where are you looking to make the biggest changes in confidence? Take some time to reflect mindfully on these questions, and write out in-depth answers below. Be sure not to censor yourself or hold back, as total honesty with yourself is the only way to truly overcome these difficulties and build lasting confidence.

Why did you pick up this book? How big of a problem is self-confidence in your life? If you gained more self-confidence, what do you think would be more resolved in your life?

MODELING SELF-CONFIDENCE

Think of self-confidence as akin to being on a spectrum instead of having it or not having it. Now think about a person in your life with a lot of self-confidence. How do you know they have self-confidence? What are the ways you have noticed or observed it in that person?

Let's focus on you. Where do you land on that spectrum of self-confidence? How do you know? What do you notice about yourself when you are feeling more confident?

Often, self-confidence comes from childhood, the support we have from adults, or the success we experience. Think about where your self-confidence—or lack of it—comes from. Do you remember having it in the past, or does it feel like it's never really been there?

What are some reasons you think you may be lacking self-confidence? If a specific painful memory or person comes to mind, take a moment to describe it/them.

How many times have you thought to yourself, I would do (blank) if I just had more confidence? How is a lack of confidence holding you back? What would you do if you had more confidence?

Trust thyself: every heart vibrates to that iron string.

– RALPH WALDO EMERSON

Reflecting on confidence is not all gloom and doom. Although it may be hard to do, take a few minutes to think about your strengths. List some of the qualities and accomplishments you are most proud of. Where do you feel the most confident in your life?

I DO HAVE STRENGTHS, AND I
DO HAVE VALUE AS A PERSON.
IT'S MY JOB TO SHOW MYSELF
TO THE WORLD.

SEEK OUT INSPIRATION

You are not on this journey alone. Many have come before you with little to no self-confidence and found ways to overcome it. In this exercise your charge is to go online and explore. Find an inspirational video about self-confidence (Brené Brown is always a good place to start—see the Resources section on page 167). Really listen to what the speaker is saying. What were the keys that helped them start their journey of change? What are some ways you can incorporate those keys into your own life?

What does true confidence feel like to you? When have you experienced it, even for a moment? Maybe it's the absence of anxiety heading into a new or stressful situation, or that feeling when you know you are prepared and about to head into a situation where you are likely to succeed.

Now that you've reflected on what confidence feels like, what experiences in your life have given your self-confidence a boost? Think about a time when you overcame a challenge or you tried something new.

Who in your life has been or could be a positive influence on your self-confidence? How has that person been helpful?

A SELF-CONFIDENCE CONVERSATION

Acknowledging your lack of confidence with another person helps decrease the shame you may feel about it. This can be a normalizing and healing process that can help motivate you and keep you on track in your journey. With whom in your life do you feel you can trust to have a conversation about self-confidence? This week, seek out that person, whether it's by text or in person, and let them know what you are dealing with. Chances are they have also experienced some of what you're going through. If there is no one you feel you can have this conversation with, just take a moment to go for a walk while acknowledging your struggles with confidence and reminding yourself that you are taking steps toward improving your self-confidence.

What barriers can you identify that are holding you back from gaining more confidence (apart from a lack of confidence)? Are these truly external, insurmountable barriers, or could they be more conceptual, cognitive, or emotional in nature?

_____

_____

_____

_____

_____

_____

_____

_____

_____

_____

_____

_____

_____

_____

_____

_____

Our natural tendency is to avoid situations that are scary and uncomfortable. Taking steps to improve your self-confidence is no different. What have you tried in the past? Did you find success, or did you end up feeling hurt or rejected in some way? Acknowledging what you've tried allows you to see better what works, what doesn't, and why it feels scary.

WHILE I WISH I HAD MORE CONFIDENCE THROUGHOUT MY LIFE, I AM NOW ON THE PATH TO GAINING THAT CONFIDENCE I HAVE ALWAYS WANTED.

What judgments and value have you placed on yourself or others regarding self-confidence? Do you think more highly of people with higher levels of confidence? What judgments do you believe everyone else holds of you because of your lack of confidence?

How much self-confidence do you think the average person has? The truth is that anxiety, self-doubt, and low self-esteem are more common than you might think. Take some time to notice your assumptions about other people's confidence. Ask yourself whether your perspective is a reality, or whether there is a chance you do not know what someone else might be struggling with.

Understand this if you understand nothing: it is a powerful thing to be seen.

— AKWAEKE EMEZI

2

SETTING YOUR GOALS

Now that you have a better sense of where you are, the next step is articulating where you want to go. This section will help you define your values—those things that matter to you most. From there, you'll work on identifying specific goals in pursuit of those values, to help you gain confidence and go after the life you want. Remember to dream big. You can always scale back your goals to more achievable and realistic levels if necessary.

WHAT DO YOU VALUE?

Let's talk values. Get in a comfortable place in your home or outside, and take several minutes to reflect on your life. What do you truly value most? What do you really want in your life, whether you currently have it or not? You might identify family, friends, career, stability, health, adventure, creativity, relaxation, or pets, to name a few. List the items in the "values" column of the table below, grouped according to how important they are to you. Then place a check mark in the column that indicates how much work that value still needs.

VALUES	GOING WELL	NEEDS SOME IMPROVEMENT	NEEDS A LOT OF IMPROVEMENT
MOST IMPORTANT			
PRETTY IMPORTANT			
LESS IMPORTANT			

WHERE TO FOCUS

Which areas need the most work? What values might you have ignored or possibly avoided due to a lack of confidence or other obstacles, whether real or perceived?

Before we get into setting goals, take a minute and check in with yourself about this process. It is normal for these prompts and exercises to cue up feelings of discomfort, shame, regret, fear, or sadness. How did it feel to identify your values?

What would it be like to truly let yourself get excited about your values? Try to allow yourself to feel some excitement, hope, and connection to these important areas of your life, whether they are going well already or could use some improvement. Describe your reactions.

_____

_____

_____

_____

_____

_____

_____

_____

_____

_____

_____

_____

_____

_____

_____

_____

_____

_____

What are some situations you know you have been avoiding due to a lack of confidence? Some examples may include social events, parties, speaking up in groups, presentations, dating, and asserting oneself at work, in public, or in home life.

We can use our values to identify goals. Looking at your list in the exercise on page 24 or the situations identified in the prompt on page 28, where do you want to start making improvements? Just pick one area to start; taking a step toward achieving one goal or objective is a great way to boost self-confidence.

I know, if it were easy to "just do it," you already would have. So how can you harness some motivation to help you get over that hump? Think for a minute about what truly motivates you. Maybe it's giving yourself an external reward, like a fun meal or a new item, or perhaps it's envisioning yourself getting to do all the things you've always wanted. Write your motivations below.

Think of a time when you set out to achieve a goal and accomplished it. What was that experience like? How did it feel?

Take a moment to reflect on how you've moved through life. You might think about graduating from high school or college, or finding a job, relationship, or other passion. What role did setting goals play in moving through each phase of life? How important were those goals in keeping you on track?

Let's spend some more time clarifying your goals. What are your *professional* goals—achievements, improvements, or ways of being in your professional life and career? These might include financial targets or specific job titles, or they could be ways of approaching your work life.

Now take some time to think through, clarify, and list your goals in your *personal* life, including relationships, family, friendships, hobbies, health, and recreational or leisure activities. An example might be improving your relationship with a sibling, or putting more time and effort into a hobby such as hiking, golfing, or playing guitar.

SET TANGIBLE GOALS

Setting goals can seem like a scary and difficult process. To assist with this, let's break your goals down into measurable, achievable, specific, and realistic actions. Take your goals from the previous prompts on pages 33 and 34 and break them down into these smaller actions. Remember to be specific. For example, "Lose weight" would be a difficult, ambiguous goal, but "exercise three times for ten minutes this week" is measurable, achievable, and realistic for many. Fill in the table below. In the column on the left, list your goal as written originally. In the column on the right, break this larger goal into one to three measurable and achievable objectives. If your original goal already fits this way, then no need to change it. If it can be broken down further to make it more manageable, break it down into smaller steps.

GOAL	SMALLER ACTION
Goal #1:	Action 1:
	Action 2:
	Action 3:
Goal #2:	Action 1:
	Action 2:
	Action 3:
Goal #3:	Action 1:
	Action 2:
	Action 3:

I learned a long time ago that there is something worse than missing the goal, and that's not pulling the trigger.

– MIA HAMM, GO FOR THE GOAL: A CHAMPION'S GUIDE TO WINNING IN SOCCER AND LIFE

What would you do if you had all the confidence in the world? Where would you go and whom would you talk to? I know this may cue up some feelings of sadness, anxiety, shame, or regret, but let's see whether there isn't also some hope, excitement, or joy in there as you consider the possibilities of a life with more confidence.

How do you think you'd interact with others if you were actively pursuing your goals and values? How do you think others would perceive you?

What limitations does your mind give you about your potential for growth? What if you were to notice that these are largely linguistic and conceptual in nature, and no one, not even your mind, can limit your growth? You are in charge of improving your life!

Your desires matter. Your values matter. You deserve to go after the life you want, and no person, thing, or feeling should take that from you. Let these words sink in. What feelings show up?

_____

_____

_____

_____

_____

_____

_____

_____

_____

_____

_____

_____

_____

_____

_____

_____

_____

_____

ACTION MUST COME BEFORE
CONFIDENCE. MY GOALS ARE
MY GUIDE TO TAKING ACTION,
WHICH WILL IN TURN BUILD
MY CONFIDENCE.

I MUST BE PATIENT AND KIND
TO MYSELF AS I BEGIN
THIS JOURNEY.

GET ACTIVE!

Give yourself a quick victory to build your confidence early in this process. Pick a goal related to physical activity. This could be taking a five-minute walk, bike ride, or jog; doing a yoga routine, stomach crunches, push-ups, or pull-ups; taking the dog on a walk or hike; getting outside and doing some yard work; or walking up and down the steps a few times in your house or somewhere nearby. It doesn't matter how big or small the task; just pick one right now that you are willing to do in this moment. Notice that your mind might already be coming up with excuses for why you can't or shouldn't, or it's not convenient timing, or you're going to get sweaty, or tired, or frustrated. We will be learning to overcome negative thoughts and self-doubts later in this journal, but for now, it will be a powerful experience for you to get out there and get a small win.

To love oneself is the beginning of a lifelong romance.

– OSCAR WILDE

3

PRACTICING SELF-ACCEPTANCE AND COMPASSION

In this section, we will begin the work of improving your self-confidence. Practicing self-acceptance and compassion is a great way to start shaping your thoughts, feelings, and experiences more positively. The foundation to confidence is truly accepting you for *you*, with all your strengths and flaws, hopes, goals, and quirks. Intentionally practicing self-love helps shift your perspective from "I can't" to "I am good enough" and "I can."

Our minds tend to drift toward the negative, critical, and judgmental. What if you were to be kinder in your self-talk, really embracing the positive, nice things about yourself? What would you say to yourself right now that would be kinder and more compassionate?

Think about a close friend or someone you care about struggling with low self-esteem and being very critical of themselves. Imagine that you can see their strengths, but they can't. What would you say to that person to help them see their true value and improve their confidence?

Most people have imposter syndrome to some degree, that is, the feeling they're not good enough at something and soon everyone will find out. Where and how is this showing up in your life? What if you were to dismiss this story as easily as you dismiss the one that you truly are special?

NOBODY'S PERFECT

Many of us struggle with the idea that we need to be striving for perfection. We feel that if we're not perfect, we're just not good enough, and we have no confidence in our ability to perform or succeed. However, successful people deal with imperfections and even outright failures all the time. The key is, the successful people are the ones willing to hang in there when they fail, and get up and try again. To drive this point home, pick your favorite athlete, musician, actor, or entrepreneur and find more information about the trials they experienced in their early career. For example, Michael Jordan famously failed to make his high school varsity basketball team sophomore year. Take notes or bookmark the information online, and go back and look at it once a week for a month to remind yourself of everyone's imperfections in life, including those with great success.

As discussed in the previous exercise (page 49), one of the biggest obstacles to self-confidence is perfectionism—believing things have to be just right or they have no value. This impossible standard can undermine your self-confidence, making you believe you've failed when you haven't. How is this a problem in your life, and what would it be like to let go of perfectionism? What would be difficult about this?

Letting go of perfection is key to boosting your self-confidence. This can be achieved, but it requires you to embrace the idea of being "good enough." What are some ways that you are actually good enough, even if you're not perfect? How does it feel to embrace this standard for yourself?

Our brains have evolved to compare ourselves to others. Early cave dwellers didn't want to be banished from the tribe for not pulling their weight! However, we don't have to be ruled by these thoughts. In what ways do you compare yourself to others? Which ones occupy the most mental time and energy for you?

Take some time to focus on more positive aspects of yourself instead of focusing on comparisons and negativity. This is not about being good at everything; rather, it's about celebrating your intrinsic value as a person and everything you have to offer the world. Reflect on this notion. What do you bring to the world?

The world deserves to get to see you and get to know you. You have positive qualities that you bring to every interaction, presentation, job, or encounter. What does it feel like to truly embrace the good you have to offer everyone? Is it easy? Difficult? A little bit of both?

I LOVE AND ACCEPT MYSELF FOR WHO I AM: ALL MY STRENGTHS, AS WELL AS MY IMPERFECTIONS.

When we embrace acceptance and positivity, our minds often come back in, reminding us of everything we have screwed up and should feel guilty and ashamed about. What situations eliciting guilt and shame are you stuck on? By approaching these situations openly and honestly, you can more easily let go of these feelings and heal.

Accept yourself, love yourself, and keep moving forward. If you want to fly, you have to give up what weighs you down.

– ROY T. BENNETT,
THE LIGHT IN THE HEART

Let's expand further on feelings of guilt or shame. Take a moment to reflect on where these feelings come from. How much of your guilt or shame is yours, and how much is put on you by others? You are allowed to push back against some of these old feelings when they no longer suit you. How does this feel?

Perhaps you are eager to see yourself in a positive light, moving forward, but your past decisions keep you stagnant because you can't seem to forgive yourself. What in your life are you unable to let go of?

PRACTICE MINDFUL BREATHING

Mindfulness can be a great tool for channeling different energy and shifting focus in your mind, especially with difficult things that make you feel stuck. For this exercise, get comfortable in your chair, and take several nice, long, deep breaths, in and out. Breathe in for three to five seconds, hold it for three to five seconds, and breathe out for three to five seconds. As you breathe in, imagine yourself breathing in compassion for yourself. Perhaps literally even repeat the words "breathing in compassion" to yourself. Hold in your breath and really take in that feeling. Then, as you breathe out, imagine breathing out judgment and shame (saying "breathing out shame"). Breathe in kindness and compassion, breathe out self-criticism. Repeat for anywhere from one to five minutes. After completing the exercise, write down your reactions in the space below.

"But wait, I'm still nervous about everything that might go wrong!" Fear not; this is completely normal. Living with uncertainty is one of the hardest things about being human. On the lines below, write about the uncertainties in life you currently fear most.

I CANNOT CONTROL EVERYTHING. I DO NOT NEED TO CONTROL EVERYTHING.

LIFE IS UNCERTAIN, AND THE JOURNEY AND THE EXPLORATION ARE PART OF WHAT MAKES IT WORTH LIVING.

CELEBRATE UNCERTAINTY!

Get creative! The goal here is to change your relationship to uncertainty itself, from one of fear to one of acceptance. Take some time to cultivate a visual image that celebrates uncertainty. You can make a picture, poster, or drawing in the space below, or find an image on your phone or computer. Try to capture several of the ways uncertainty comes out in life, from relationships and jobs to health and recreation. You can even make a vision board, with a collage of pictures, photos, words, phrases, or anything that jumps out at you and allows you to dance with uncertainty.

Another tool for improving positivity, acceptance, and confidence is practicing gratitude. When do you have gratitude in your life? What people, things, circumstances, or memories are you grateful for having or experiencing?

PRACTICE GRATITUDE

Using your ideas from the previous entry, let's set an active goal around practicing gratitude. Write an email per week for a month to someone you are grateful to. Additionally, every day, write down one thing you are grateful for in a gratitude log. It can be a person, thing, situation, or something else. Every two weeks, go back through and reread your log entries about everything you have to be grateful for. You might find you have more in your life than you realize, which will help build your confidence.

Consider for a moment these simple questions: Whom are you living your life for? Whose dreams and values matter most to you? It's so easy to get caught up in the pressures of keeping up with others or achieving titles or life "successes" based on values determined by someone else—without even realizing it. If the answer to these questions isn't "me" or "mine," take a moment to shift that priority back to yourself. Write about your values here.

CONNECT IT ALL TOGETHER

Hopefully now the connections among self-acceptance, self-love, and self-confidence are starting to make sense. To illustrate this, fill in the chart on the next page connecting the three boxes of self-acceptance, self-love, and self-confidence. In the acceptance and love boxes, begin by writing a few qualities, traits, or accomplishments that exemplify what you accept and love about yourself. Next, add a few ideas to each box indicating what you can do to practice self-acceptance and self-love on a daily basis. Then look at how the foundation of self-acceptance and self-love can lead to more self-confidence in different areas or in different qualities about yourself. List those words in the confidence box. For example, you might write things like:

"I accept my slower thought process in conversations."

"I treat myself to a fun meal once a week to practice self-love."

"My personality is something to have confidence in, not anxiety/shame about, in social interactions."

FOUNDATION OF SELF-CONFIDENCE

SELF-CONFIDENCE

SELF-ACCEPTANCE

SELF-LOVE

The past has no power over the present moment.

– ECKHART TOLLE

4

CALMING YOUR BODY
TO CALM YOUR MIND

This section is all about using your body to build confidence. We will discuss important ideas and strategies for calming your body as well as conveying confident body language to decrease your stress and present your best self in a situation. It's hard to feel confident mentally when you're not taking care of things physically. Subtle changes can have a powerful effect, focusing your attention on the things that matter and helping you succeed, leading to more confidence over time.

Think back to any interpersonal interactions you've had over the last week. Take a moment to reflect on your body language, such as your standing, posture, facial expressions, eye contact, or arm position. What messages do you think you convey to the world? What messages would you like to be conveying?

At this point, you may not feel confident in every part of your body language. That's okay; many people don't. By increasing self-awareness of how you come across, you can make the changes that will boost self-confidence. What aspects of your body language display confidence versus a lack of confidence?

NOTICE YOUR WORLD

Eye contact is one of the most important ways to display confidence, which will, in turn, signal confidence back to your brain. In order to maintain eye contact, you must be looking up and out at the world and the people you interact with. Over the next week, every time you leave your house and are walking somewhere, whether it's from your car to a store or office or somewhere else, take note of your surroundings. When you get to your destination, pause a minute and see how many details you can remember about your journey. Whom did you pass by? What did they look like? Were there trees, cars, buildings, or something else around? This exercise will help you be more present-moment focused and remind you to keep your head up and notice and engage with the world around you.

Picture someone in your life who is extremely confident. What do they look like? What kind of body language do they exhibit? Where are their eyes, shoulders, arms, hands, etc.?

Let's get explicit about your body language. Using the table below, every day for a week, check off the behavior(s) you made a point to do when you were out in public or around other people. The primary ones to focus on are:

posture—standing or sitting up straight

shoulders back and relaxed

arms at your side, or moving naturally with an activity or when speaking

hands relaxed and not fidgeting, not touching your face or hair

head and chin up

maintaining comfortable eye contact

relaxed smile, but not overly eager or forced

looking to others to imitate similar body language

The goal is to do all of these every day in every situation, but the real success will be increasing awareness and intention of doing these more consistently.

BEHAVIOR	SUN	MON	TUES	WED	THURS	FRI	SAT
Posture							
Shoulders back							
Arms							
Hands down							
Head up							
Eye contact							
Smile							
Imitating others							

Now that you're conveying more confident body language, the next aspect of confidence is staying present to reduce stress and increase comfort in your body. Take a moment. Where is your mind right now? Is it focused on this book, or is it somewhere else? What stories are you caught up in that keep you out of the present?

Mindfulness is all about staying present, nonjudgmentally, allowing all the thoughts, feelings, and sensations that show up on the inside, while at the same time staying engaged with the external situation and your environment. How do you feel about this idea? What feels scary about this? What feels hopeful?

PRACTICE MINDFULNESS

Mindfulness has been practiced for thousands of years as a way of accepting, and thereby letting go of, unpleasant and anxious thoughts and feelings. Most likely, if you've picked up this journal, you have been experiencing these on a regular basis as they chip away at your self-confidence. Practice staying present and just describing what is there. If you are able, take a mindful walk. Walk for ten minutes outside, noticing your surroundings: the sights, smells, and sounds, and what the air feels like. Focus on your senses rather than on your thoughts or judgments about what you notice. Try to just take in the experience, nonverbally. Confidence comes when you are truly comfortable with things just as they are. Practice this with your environment so you can learn how to apply it to yourself.

Shift your focus now to thinking about your stress responses. What do you do when you're experiencing a stressful moment or interaction? Fidget? Look away? Look at your phone? Excuse yourself from the situation or run to the bathroom? These are likely all behaviors acting to help you avoid your distress. Write out your tendencies here. What would it be like to limit these responses and sit with the discomfort instead?

SQUARE BREATHING

Another way to calm yourself is to practice steady breathing. Knowing that you can generally keep your breathing under control will help you gain confidence going into a challenging situation. Sit in a comfortable place, close your eyes, and place your hand on your belly. Breathe in for four to five seconds and hold it about a second, then breathe out for four to five seconds and pause for one to two seconds before taking your next breath. Allow your belly to expand on the inhales and contract on the exhales. While you breathe, visualize drawing a square. Draw one side as you inhale, pause at the corner, then draw the next side as you exhale. Draw the third side on the inhale, and complete the square with the exhale. Practice this for at least two minutes per day when you are feeling calm. Then pull it out as needed when feeling more stressed.

I AM FOCUSED AND READY TO
PRESENT MYSELF CONFIDENTLY
TO THE WORLD.

What else do you do to soothe yourself during moments of stress? This could include healthy behaviors such as going for a walk or doing deep breathing, or less healthy behaviors such as drinking alcohol or smoking cigarettes. Write down a few ways you currently soothe yourself. Then make a new list of more positive behaviors you could choose.

What do you do on a regular basis to relax and stay de-stressed? Do you read, watch shows or movies, walk your dog, play music? Evaluate these habits and write about why you choose them.

Taking care of your body is of the utmost importance for reducing stress—helping you feel more relaxed and increasing your confidence throughout the week. Take a moment to honestly reflect on the three main areas of diet, exercise, and sleep. How are you doing in each area? How does it feel? How would you like things to be?

PRACTICE SELF-CARE

As you may notice, a running theme in this journal and many workbooks is consistency. Try committing to practicing and improving one realm of self-care each week for the next five weeks. You can pick the order, but the five categories will be:

mindfulness/staying present

self-soothing

nutrition and diet

sleep

exercise

Your focus will shift from week to week, but be sure to continue some maintenance practice in each area. At the end of the five weeks, you should begin to build in these practices more consistently. You can choose the specific exercises from ideas in this journal or come up with new ones. There is a wealth of information online for mindfulness exercises, calming exercises, meal-planning and nutrition, and sleep hygiene. Throughout each week, keep a log of what you did and how it went so you can see what you like and what fits well for you.

WEEK 1:

WEEK 2:

WEEK 3:

_____

_____

_____

_____

_____

WEEK 4:

_____

_____

_____

_____

_____

WEEK 5:

_____

_____

_____

_____

_____

It's important to check in on the impact of drugs and alcohol in your life. These substances, including nicotine, can have significant effects on your physical and mental health and well-being. Take some time to reflect honestly on what role these substances play in your life, how you feel about that, and what changes you might consider making in this area.

We can complain because rose bushes have thorns, or rejoice because thorns have roses.

— ALPHONSE KARR

5

CHALLENGING NEGATIVE THOUGHTS AND BELIEFS

This section is all about challenging your negative thoughts and core beliefs about yourself that are feeding and maintaining your low self-confidence. The approach here is a combination of not fearing your negative thoughts, accepting any discomfort they may be pointing to, and really knocking out the ones that have no basis and are not useful. While we are never without our thoughts, our thoughts do not have to define us, control us, or limit us.

What are the five most prevalent negative thoughts impacting your confidence today?

How do your five negative thoughts relate to your self-confidence? How big an impact do they have on your confidence and why?

IDENTIFY NEGATIVE THOUGHTS

When combating negative thoughts, organizing and categorizing them can help you understand them better. In this exercise, let's look at the types of negative thoughts that seem to be impacting you the most. How much are you dwelling on the following themes? Rank the themes below in order of most relevant to least relevant. Then write out one of your negative beliefs or thoughts related to that theme, so that you can see it, know it, and tackle it.

Past mistakes   I don't measure up   Lazy

Current abilities   Unattractive   Dumb

Hopeless future   No talent   Not good enough

Boring   Unlovable   Other

Others don't like me

THEME

RELATED NEGATIVE THOUGHT

What kind of negative thought patterns do you notice yourself getting stuck in? Do you find yourself thinking about things in an "all or nothing" way? Do you assume other people are judging you or that you know what they're thinking? Do you take personally everything that others say? When these thoughts come, how do you typically respond to them?

THOUGHTS ARE JUST THOUGHTS. MY NEGATIVE THOUGHTS ARE NOT TRUE OR FAIR REPRESENTATIONS OF MY ABILITY TO SUCCEED.

Think about someone in your life or on TV who seems to have a positive outlook. How do they reframe things to be more positive? How do they come across in terms of positive mood or self-confidence?

Why do you think you trust your negative thoughts? What about them makes you believe them to be true?

What are some effective ways you've coped with negative thoughts in the past? If you'd like to improve on this, think about some confidence-building ways you can cope in the future. Some ideas could include trying to look at your thoughts differently or more positively, engaging in positive activities such as journaling or exercising, or seeking support and comfort from others.

REFRAME NEGATIVE BELIEFS

It's time to reframe some of your negative thoughts into more useful ones. This will help build your self-confidence. In the left-hand column below, write out five to ten negative thoughts you have been struggling with. On the right side, write out a more positive reframe for each thought. Some ideas for reframes include thinking of past failures or current struggles as opportunities to grow or learn and remembering that one thing going wrong or one person not liking you is not indicative of all people not liking you or all things going wrong.

A specific example looks like this:

"I'll never find a romantic partner." Vs. "I am making small changes to work toward my goal."

NEGATIVE THOUGHTS	POSITIVE REFRAME

We all have an inner critic that tells us that we're not good enough in various ways and that we shouldn't strive too much for fear of failure and disappointment. Imagine acknowledging this voice and then putting it in the back of your mind with the volume turned down. Think of yourself as the driver of your life, and this inner critic as merely a passenger. How does this feel?

Life is either a daring adventure or nothing.

– HELEN KELLER, LET US HAVE FAITH

Self-doubt functions to "keep us safe" by encouraging us to avoid potentially painful situations or outcomes. But the truth is you don't need to be kept safe. The pain of disappointment, failure, and rejection is temporary. The pain of avoiding pursuing your goals lasts as long as you avoid. Challenge your mind to focus more on positive outcomes than on failures. Reflect on this idea of no longer being bullied by self-doubt.

I WILL NOT FEAR MY NEGATIVE THOUGHTS. I KNOW THEY ARE NOT TRUE, AND I AM STRONG ENOUGH TO GO AFTER THE LIFE I WANT, DESPITE WHAT THEY SAY.

PUSH BACK AGAINST SELF-DOUBT

Self-doubt feeds on the idea that you are too fragile and can't handle negative outcomes. This is NOT true! For this exercise, pick three self-doubts. For each self-doubt, answer the question "And then what will happen?" multiple times. The goal is to help you dig deeper and deeper into what you are actually worried about. Often the fear is something that is either irrational or highly unlikely. Or it is something that is really not that dangerous or harmful. Try to answer the question of what will happen at least three to five times for each doubt. Then evaluate just how bad these outcomes are, how likely they are, and whether you really need to pay so much attention to the self-doubt in your head.

Self-doubt #1

_____

_____

What's the worst that can happen?

_____

_____

_____

_____

Self-doubt #2

_____

_____

What's the worst that can happen?

_____

_____

_____

_____

Self-doubt #3

_____

_____

What's the worst that can happen?

_____

_____

_____

_____

Core beliefs have usually been with us since childhood, but they may not be relevant now. An example might be a parent or teacher who tells you that you will never amount to anything, or a bully who calls you a loser. What core beliefs do you hold about yourself? How long have you held them? Where do they come from?

To build self-confidence, we must challenge our negative core beliefs. One way is to challenge the source where they came from. Another is to challenge the conclusions drawn from limited evidence earlier in life. Notice that core beliefs usually discount any positive thing you have achieved that contradicts the core belief. Reflect on these ideas, and write out some reasons why these negative core beliefs should not be trusted.

Negative core beliefs can come from people who, for their own reasons, acted in ways that hurt you. They did not truly know you then or see the whole you, they don't know you now, and they certainly don't know what you're capable of. Think of a person who may have hurt you, and write them a positive reframe of yourself that highlights why they were wrong and how you have grown.

USE HUMOR TO QUIET NEGATIVE THOUGHTS

It's common to struggle with negative thoughts. Wouldn't it be great if we could just make them go away entirely? The good news is that you can change your relationship to your thoughts. Thoughts are just a jumble of words that your mind throws at you. Try taking them a little less seriously. To do this, think of one negative thought. Now, instead of just saying it to yourself, try singing the thought to the tune of "Happy Birthday." This may seem ridiculous, but that's the point—hearing these thoughts as the ridiculous, untrue things that they are gives you some choice in how they impact you. It's harder to take a self-critical thought seriously when it's being sung to a fun tune. You can also say it in a funny famous person's voice, such as Arnold Schwarzenegger's, or repeat the thought as a little ant or mouse. Practice this for a few minutes twice a week with any thoughts that are particularly hard to manage.

Now that you've identified some old core beliefs that likely aren't very helpful, let's get to work on establishing new core beliefs that will help you gain confidence. Think about your work, education, or hobbies. What skills, knowledge, and accomplishments do you have? What would you be capable of if you pushed yourself further?

In the realm of relationships, friendships, family, and interpersonal situations, think of some successes. Whom are you happy to have in your life? What kind of people are you confident you could connect with moving forward?

It's helpful to understand the relationship between negative thoughts, core beliefs, and self-confidence. How does it feel to think about heading into a challenging situation with more positive beliefs about yourself and your ability to handle things? Reflect on and write about the idea of shedding this wet, heavy, negative blanket and living a freer, more confident life.

What are the statements you want to define you moving forward? What values are they based on? What do you want to believe about yourself, even if it still feels difficult right now to fully embrace it and believe it?

DECLARE POSITIVE AFFIRMATIONS

Write out seven positive affirmations that contribute to more self-confidence. Examples include statements about skills or qualities that make you a good worker, student, friend, partner, parent, or neighbor. For each day of the week, take one minute and read one of these assertively, out loud in front of the mirror—a declaration to the world about who you are and what you offer. Notice your body language as you say these statements. Be sure to project confidence to yourself and others through both your actions and your words.

MONDAY:

_____

_____

_____

TUESDAY:

_____

_____

_____

WEDNESDAY:

_____

_____

_____

THURSDAY:

_____

_____

_____

FRIDAY:

_____

_____

_____

SATURDAY:

_____

_____

_____

SUNDAY:

_____

_____

_____

Remember that confidence does not mean you eliminate every negative thought. Confidence is facing the negative thoughts and deciding not to listen to them. Imagine you are a coach giving yourself a pep talk going into a challenging event. What can you say to yourself to build up your confidence?

No kind of life is worth leading if it is always an easy life.

— THEODORE ROOSEVELT

6

FACING YOUR FEARS AND DOUBTS

We are wired to avoid dangers, so it's no surprise that fears and doubts lead us to avoid situations where we perceive the potential for failure, humiliation, or disappointment. The good news is you can overcome these fears through direct action, determination, and willingness. Self-confidence comes not just from successes but also from handling setbacks, learning from mistakes, and pushing forward toward your valued goals in the face of self-doubt and fear.

Growth is not always comfortable, but it is always possible. How do you feel about this idea?

What insecurities are holding you back? Are you afraid of getting hurt, afraid of failing, afraid of disappointing others, or afraid of disappointing yourself?

Life can be exhausting, especially if you have experienced several setbacks, failures, or disappointments time and again. Give yourself permission today to just sit in and reflect on the struggles you have experienced. Your feelings are valid. Write out some of them here.

In the previous prompt (page 124), you focused on your setbacks. Now let's move forward. Where is that ember of hope in you? What does it want? What does it believe could be possible and worth going after, even if it means facing something scary?

To free you from the chains of self-doubt, it's important to get closure on past failures in relationships, jobs, school, or friendships. Reflect on any open wounds from the past. What still needs to be done for you to heal? Write out compassionate, forgiving statements to yourself for these past painful experiences to truly put them behind you.

Patience is key to growth and developing confidence. Progress and success will not happen overnight. Do you resist being patient? Embrace the idea of being more patient with yourself. How does this feel?

I AM ON THE RIGHT PATH TO BUILDING MY CONFIDENCE.

IF I STICK WITH THIS, I WILL GAIN CONFIDENCE AND GET THE LIFE I WANT AND AM CAPABLE OF LIVING.

As mentioned, avoidance and fear go hand in hand. Be honest with yourself. Regarding relationships, friendships, and interpersonal interactions, what are you avoiding, and what fear is this related to?

Take another honest look, this time at the realm of education, job, and career. What are you avoiding, and what is your fear?

Regarding personal health, growth, hobbies, or fitness, what are your avoidance behaviors, and what do you fear?

The opposite of avoidance is exposure—committed action toward valued goals. This might elicit some anxiety if you are afraid of failure. But take a moment to reflect on how it would feel to really embrace a life of exposure and action instead of avoidance. Write about the details—your feelings and your actions—here.

Sometimes we figure out ways to get to a difficult situation, but then our lack of confidence leads to safety-seeking behaviors once we're there. These might include staying quiet at a social event or business meeting, avoiding eye contact, or staying on our phone and not really interacting. What safety behaviors do you notice yourself engaging in?

TAKE THE FIRST STEPS

The key to any effective action plan is breaking big goals into small, attainable steps. Identify one area you have been avoiding because of fear and write it in the lines under "Area." Then, under "Goal," write down one goal you would like to accomplish in this realm. Finally, break that goal into smaller steps, and write those in the lines under "Steps." For example, maybe you've avoided pursuing romantic relationships for fear of rejection. That would be the area to focus on. The goal would be meeting someone new and starting a relationship. The smaller steps might include downloading a dating app, setting up a profile, and talking to friends or others and expressing some interest in dating.

AREA

_____

_____

_____

_____

_____

_____

_____

GOAL

_____

_____

_____

_____

_____

_____

_____

STEPS

_____

_____

_____

_____

_____

_____

_____

_____

_____

_____

Failure is growth, and growth comes from failure. Accepting this means truly embracing it and allowing for the possibility of failure. Self-confidence comes from believing you will get through it, no matter the consequences, and giving yourself repeated opportunities for success. What is the hardest part to accept about this concept?

You may not control all the events that happen to you, but you can decide not to be reduced by them.

— MAYA ANGELOU

CONFRONT FAILURE

Let's take another look at the idea of failure not harming you. Think back through some past failures to see whether there is more to the story than just a fear of it happening again. Reflect on a time when you failed, then answer these questions.

What happened?

_____

_____

_____

What were the worst consequences?

_____

_____

_____

Were they justified?

_____

_____

_____

How long did the consequences actually affect your life? How long did they affect your thoughts or feelings?

_____

_____

_____

What did you learn from the experience?

_____

_____

_____

What other opportunities did you explore subsequently that you might not have if you had "succeeded" in the first endeavor?

_____

_____

_____

Was it a complete and utter failure? Were there any parts that weren't so bad? Did any positives come from this?

_____

_____

_____

FAILURE CANNOT HARM ME. IT IS PAINFUL IN THE MOMENT, BUT I AM STRONG ENOUGH TO HANDLE IT AND NOT BE HELD BACK BY A FEAR OF THINGS GOING WRONG.

Dwelling on fears and doubts can lead to stress over time. Conversely, getting little victories from taking on small exposures and achieving small goals will have a positive snowball effect. How does it feel to embrace a more positive, "I can" outlook? How does it feel to have some successes?

The point of taking action is not only to accomplish things but also to reinforce that things will get better and that you can do challenging things. Write five statements of hope, reminding yourself that things will get better.

LET YOUR THOUGHTS FLOAT BY

To deal with troublesome fears, doubts, and stressful thoughts, it is helpful to try to notice them and let them go. In this mindfulness exercise, imagine yourself sitting on the edge of a stream in a peaceful forest. As a stressful thought about failure, rejection, or not being good enough pops into your mind, picture yourself placing the thought on a leaf in the stream and watching it float on by. Sit for five minutes, imagining yourself by the stream, and continuously place your thoughts on leaves and watch them float away. Do this with every thought, noticing that you are not your thoughts or ruled by your thoughts. See that they come and go and don't stick around forever. Practice this exercise as often as you wish throughout the month.

Building confidence does not have to happen alone. Who is on your team in this journey? Whom do you want to enlist? What feelings show up when you think about enlisting some support in your journey?

GET A PARTNER IN CRIME

We have talked a lot about taking action toward your goals to build confidence. It is perfectly acceptable and often beneficial to enlist a friend when taking on a new challenge or encountering a new situation. Your job is to pick a goal, identify a support person, and ask them to support you in some way. For example, have a friend come with you to a new group, club, singles event, job fair, networking event, audition, or bar. Or you can schedule a time to talk or hang out with a friend before or after the anxiety-provoking event so you can get a pep talk or debrief with them. Text with them heading into an event to get a last-minute confidence boost. You don't have to do this all alone. Also consider seeking out help from a therapist or mental health professional.

Only those who dare to fail greatly, can ever achieve greatly.

– ROBERT F. KENNEDY

7

MOVING FORWARD WITH CONFIDENCE

Hopefully by now, you are starting to develop some healthier habits and building your confidence. The key to making real change is practice and persistence. There will be successes and setbacks throughout your life. Confidence will wax and wane accordingly, but you have gained control over how much you let those disappointments set you back, versus staying on course and coming back stronger the next time. This section is about solidifying your hard-earned progress moving forward.

It's natural for your mind to race ahead to things that might go wrong. You don't need to fear ideas about the future. Face your fear. What is your mind racing ahead to—specific events or a general fear about the future?

STAY PRESENT

One strategy for reducing anxiety and maintaining confidence in the moment is to stay present. Our minds want to look out for the next danger ahead. Instead, when faced with a tough situation, ground yourself in the present in order to calm yourself. To practice this, check in with yourself every day. Take a deep breath and just notice what is happening, both internally and in your outside environment. You can notice your thoughts about the future without being ruled by them. You can bring your focus and awareness back to the people and things around you in the moment, which are usually less scary than the ideas you have about them in your mind.

Remember the healthy habits, such as mindfulness and self-care, that we talked about in chapter 4 (page 71)? Take a look at your lists from that chapter. For these to be maximally effective, they need regular practice. Why will you continue to do them? Why is it important to you?

Think of the healthy habits you've been practicing. Which are you most excited about? Picture yourself a few months down the road having put these habits into regular practice. Maybe you've started exercising regularly or using more confident body language in interpersonal situations. What changes might you notice in yourself? How will that feel?

PRACTICE HEALTHY HABITS

Not to sound like a broken record here, but once again, let's emphasize the importance of practicing good habits. Good habits take time and repetition to build. Confidence will grow as you build these habits and reap the benefits of feeling better. Get out your calendar. Look at the next two weeks. Make sure you are blocking out time for physical activity, socializing, and planning at least a few healthy meals throughout your week. Also, be sure your schedule allows for proper sleep at relatively similar times each night, getting at least seven to eight hours. Last, remember your body language strategies. These need to be practiced every single day! Choose one confidence-building body language behavior to work on every day. This could be eye contact, head up, shoulders back, open stance, or reduced fidgeting.

Write out some of your long-term goals. Dream big here. Think about where you want to be 5, 10, or 20 years down the road. How will self-confidence play a role in this?

While considering long-term goals, also remember it's about the journey as much as the destination, as that is where you'll be spending a lot of time. What will you appreciate about this journey? What will help you stay present during the journey?

_____

_____

_____

_____

_____

_____

_____

_____

_____

_____

_____

_____

_____

_____

_____

_____

_____

_____

Setbacks and disappointments are part of the journey. Part of building confidence is being ready to face these setbacks, deal with them, and learn from them. Anticipating them ahead of time can make them less scary. What setbacks do you anticipate happening as you build your confidence and go after new things? What emotions come up for you when you think about this?

Don't be discouraged by disappointments. What can you tell yourself to provide comfort during these times? How can you encourage yourself through these difficult phases of building confidence?

Cockiness and overconfidence are potential pitfalls on this journey. Take a moment now to reflect on any areas in which you may be feeling overconfident. What do you think is behind this? What is a more effective way to approach these situations, where you can balance confidence with some humility?

KEEP TRACK OF SELF-CARE HABITS

A big part of taking on any new challenge is practicing self-care to keep you feeling rested, restored, and motivated. Remember to do things for yourself and take care of your health. When you feel better physically and mentally, you boost your confidence in any situation. Self-care takes intentional practice. On the lines below, write out at least one self-care practice you will complete each week over the next four weeks. At the end of four weeks, repeat this exercise for the next four weeks. The time and duration of the self-care activity does not matter. Just make sure it gets done.

WEEK 1:

_____

_____

WEEK 2:

_____

_____

WEEK 3:

_____

_____

WEEK 4:

_____

_____

Another key to building and maintaining self-confidence is your willingness to say "no" to people. Sometimes you may not want to do something, and it will build your confidence to be honest with yourself and others when this happens. What is the scariest or hardest part about this? How do you imagine it will feel to be assertive about your needs?

Patience is bitter, but its fruit is sweet.

– JEAN CHARDIN

Patience is paramount. There are no guarantees for when you will start feeling more confident or exactly what the road will look like. The good news is that patience is a choice. You have it even if you don't think you do. How does this feel? What feelings are hard for you to tolerate and lead to impatience for you?

I WILL BE PATIENT WITH MYSELF FOR AS LONG AS THIS JOURNEY TAKES. I AM CONFIDENT I CAN HANDLE THE OBSTACLES AND PERSEVERE TO ACHIEVE MY GOALS.

When you really start acting more confident, others will notice, and you may even serve as a role model to them! Your confidence will be contagious and help others who may be struggling with similar issues. How does it feel to potentially be a role model in this way?

Of the confidence-building activities you have tried so far, which one is your favorite? Reflect on this and how it's gone and the impact it has had on your growth.

What has surprised you about this journey of building confidence up to this point? What have you learned about yourself?

A FINAL WORD

Congratulations and thank you for making it this far! I hope that you have begun to notice the changes in yourself and your confidence. Self-confidence is about pushing yourself to pursue the things you want, regardless of the anxieties that show up. You are the captain of your life. It is up to you to identify what matters to you and take real steps in those valued directions. I promise that if you take meaningful steps toward your goals, you will feel a sense of accomplishment and fulfillment that can build confidence and happiness throughout your life.

Let's review the main confidence-building ideas to continue working on. Present strong, open, confident body language when you walk into any situation. This includes having your chin up, smiling, making eye contact, and speaking in a clear voice.

When the negative thoughts show up, do not listen to them or get bogged down by them. They don't know the whole story, they can't tell the future, and they don't know what you're truly capable of. When you start worrying about what everyone else thinks, or how you might fail, simply respond internally, "Who cares? I can handle this." Take pride in who you are!

And remember, confidence is built primarily through actions. The more action you take, the more opportunities you have for success, which will build confidence over time. If you get discouraged, you can always take breaks or seek support from friends, family, or professionals.

RESOURCES

Below is a list of books, websites, and other resources to help you gain further insight and support on your journey.

BOOKS:

Companion workbook with useful exercises to build self-confidence:
Markway, Barbara, and Celia Ampel. *The Self-Confidence Workbook: A Guide to Overcoming Self-Doubt and Improving Self-Esteem*. Althea Press, 2018.

ACT-based book with good explanations of concepts and ideas for overcoming anxiety:
Harris, Russ. *The Confidence Gap: A Guide to Overcoming Fear and Self-Doubt.* Trumpeter, 2011.

ACT-based book with more mindfulness approaches mixed in for dealing with anxiety:
Wilson, Kelly G., and Troy DuFrene. *Things Might Go Terribly, Horribly Wrong: A Guide to Life Liberated from Anxiety*. New Harbinger Publications, 2010.

ORGANIZATIONS:

Organization with regular meetings to build confidence in public speaking:
Toastmasters.org

This site has many public social groups based on several activities and themes where you can meet new people in your area:
Meetup.com

Search for therapists in your area who take your insurance and say they work with anxiety and/or self-esteem and self-confidence issues:
PsychologyToday.com

WEBSITES:

This website has many videos of Brené Brown discussing topics from self-confidence to shame and vulnerability. Additional videos and interviews can be found on YouTube.com.
BreneBrown.com

This website has lots of good information on improving oneself:
PositivePsychology.com/category/the-self

This website has online classes on several topics including building confidence specifically. Free trial available:
Skillshare.com

This site has many useful Dialectical Behavior Therapy handouts and trainings, including ones on interpersonal effectiveness, which will help build confidence in interpersonal interactions:
DBTSelfHelp.com

ABOUT THE AUTHOR

DR. DAVID SHANLEY is a psychologist in private practice in Denver, Colorado. He earned a BA from the University of Pennsylvania and his PsyD from the University of Denver. He specializes in the treatment of anxiety disorders and helps clients gain confidence by pursuing their values. Gaining self-confidence has been a lifelong journey that Dr. Shanley continues to pursue through his work and personal life. He is the author of two other books on overcoming anxiety (*The Social Anxiety Workbook for Work, Public and Social Life* and *Overcoming Panic Attacks*). He is fortunate to have supportive family and friends who have helped push him to go after the things he wants in life. He finds that the outdoors have always offered an opportunity for fun, positive challenges and adventures.